DRIVERS'
DILEMMAS

Outrageous and Bizarre Journal Entries
Between a Driver and a Recruiter

Jeremy Mincke

Table of Contents

Dedication

This book is dedicated to each and every CDL Driver (Commercial Driver Licensed Driver) out there. We are able to feed our families, get our necessities, and all our precious needs and wants are delivered right to our doors and stores because of you. I enjoy each of you and have been blessed by meeting many of you daily. I thank you for your services and, most of all, your friendships.

— Jeremy and the CDL Hunter Family

Foreword

Recruiting is all about people, and people are hilarious. There's nothing like the pressure of a job interview to bring out the most awkward, silly, and mystifying behavior in all of us.

While we often celebrate the victories — like a perfect referral, nailing your dream job search on the first try, or the perfect candidate saying yes as soon as they are offered the job — let's take some time to share a few of the most comical and unusual interactions that Driver Recruiting has to offer along with those victories.

Let's Start in the Year 2015

Spring of 2015

Recruiting manager: Your driver from Mississippi didn't show up today, Mincke!

Me: Really?

(His remark, however, wasn't a surprise. I knew that he would be checking since we got the driver a rental car instead of a Greyhound ticket. Car Rentals and plane tickets are added hiring expenses, so a carrier / manager will always pay close attention to the hiring progress for these drivers.)

Recruiting manager: Nope... and neither did our rental car, which we confirmed was picked up Friday by *your* driver!

Me: Oh, great...

Two days passed and nothing, no driver and no rental car. On Wednesday morning, I found my recruiting manager at my desk even before my first cup of coffee. He had that we-got-another-crazy-one-on-our-hands look on his face.

Recruiting manager: Well, we located the rental car along with the driver who was found yesterday morning in a flop house. He was passed plum out on an old mattress, high as a kite on some crack. The rental car was recovered a few hours ago, so we're kind of good on that front. Can you believe he actually traded a car worth thousands of dollars for some crack!

What can I say? There's never a dull moment on the recruiting floor.

The Accident

The summer of 2015 had just kicked off.

A current driver and friend of mine, who I will call "Bill", called the office sounding very anxious.

Before we really get into it, here's a little backstory on Bill. He is a driver I've known and worked with for many years, placing him in various jobs throughout his career. We spoke so often about life outside of driving that we became good friends. He has a strong, drawn out stammer, so often it takes him a while to get through sentences. However, we have such great conversations that you quickly forget about it and could talk to him all day. So, with that said, let's get back to Bill and his accident.

Bill: I was headed down 40, cruising along, when a vehicle that was on the side of the road pulled onto the highway right in front of me. There was nothing I could do but hit him. Luckily, I was in my 4-wheeler — which is trucker lingo for a personal or civilian vehicle — and not my big truck, or the guy would be dead.

Me: Wait, what? Bill, did this just happen?

Bill: Ha! Yes, Sir, about twenty minutes ago. Lucky guy, he's fine, but his truck's not and I don't think his mind will be either.

He was laughing hysterically at this point, and I wasn't sure if it was due to stress or something else. I hoped there was something really funny that he was about to tell me.

Me: Slow down, Bill, take a breath. Are you okay? Are the police and paramedics on the way?

Bill continued: I hit him so hard that I lost my legs. Both of them! Can you believe it?

So, I got out of my truck, which actually ended up in front of the vehicle I hit, and proceeded to crawl arm-over-arm towards him. That's when I saw his eyes, big as silver dollars, staring at me in shock. Now that I think about it, he probably thought he was in a scene from The Walking Dead! I'm surprised he didn't flat pass out, LOL. I mean, I was shouting at him as I crawled, asking if he was okay and if he'd seen my legs! Can you believe it? I actually asked him about my missing legs, LOL! Anyway, the highway patrol found my legs. They were both in his truck!

I need to clarify that "Bill" is a double amputee. The first people on the scene found his prosthetic legs in the other vehicle. Had they still been his real legs, he would have lost them a second time. I was flattered that he called me, but advised him to get some rest, go to the hospital, and call me tomorrow.

Jump into 2016

Spring of 2016

I'll never forget the day that one of my new recruiters, who I will call "Wayne," popped his head up over his cubicle and said: "Well, my first driver took the bus to his orientation!"

Me: That's great, Wayne, keep it up!

Wayne: Well, yes it would be, except that somewhere along the route to orientation he got a call from home that his fish had died. So, when he got off the bus, he decided to just head right back home to bury his fish.

Me: Really?

Wayne: Yup, and he is on the phone right now asking to come back.

Me: Well, get him back down there and get him to work! He has a funeral to pay for!

10/12/2016

Me: Joe, your travel schedule is set, so we'll see you Monday!

Joe: Sorry, Sir, but I have to reschedule.

Me: Reschedule? Why?

Joe: Well, Sir, we just discovered that my wife is pregnant.

Me: Oh, congrats! That's no problem. You will be home plenty of times over the next six to nine months to go to appointments, shop for baby stuff, paint the baby's room, and all that fun stuff!

Joe: Well, the problem is that she's due in two weeks.

Me: She's due in two weeks! Wait, you all just found out?

Joe: Yes, Sir. We didn't know. We actually had no idea she was pregnant at all.

Me: So, it seems like you guys don't really see each other much. We definitely have to get you on a job with more home time! Can't imagine she'd kept it from you like a really big surprise! LOL.

Joe: No, man, she didn't know at all. Neither of us did!

Me: How does someone not know that they're pregnant for nine months? It doesn't make any sense, I don't understand.

Joe: It just blended with her body, man. You know how it is.

Me: Um, well okay, Joe, call me after the baby comes and congrats again!

11/16/2016

This morning I called one of my drivers with whom I've developed a great relationship. I had actually gotten him started in the industry as a CDL Driver many years ago. In fact, now when we speak, which is quite often, it's more about life and rarely trucking.

This morning, his sister, Tammy, answered his cell phone which is very unusual. I knew he had been off the last few weeks, but he should have been back out on the road in his truck. I also knew he had been at his mother's for home time and not his sister's.

Tammy proceeded to tell me that Mark had passed away from a heart attack on Saturday in his home. I was in shock. He was only thirty years old!

I know he would want me to share part of
his story here. He was overweight when we
first met, and I'd book him two seats to
fly to orientations. He started an "on the
road" fitness program and changed his diet
dramatically. I think that getting in and
out of the truck proved to be tough and
the more weight he lost the better he felt,
naturally. He had made a lot of progress
shaving off hundreds of pounds and
started helping others do the same.

Mark will be missed and this morning was a
sobering reminder to take care of
ourselves, that life is short, and to not
take any days for granted.

"Your shift is over driver, thank you for
being my friend."

The Year 2017

02/06/2017

Me: Jose, I saw that you left orientation last Monday, January 23rd.

Jose: Yeah, I ended up going home because the shuttle was late to get me.

Me: Did you call the shuttle when you got there?

Jose: Nah. I just had some stuff I had to take care of at home so I couldn't wait around.

Me: Jose, it's the 5th — the 5th of February. No one could locate you. Not even your wife.

Jose: Yeah, I'm pretty tired. I just walked back home.

Me: You walked from Atlanta to Tampa?

Jose: [silence]

Me: Jose, you still there?

Jose's wife [picks up the phone]: Jose fell asleep talking to you. And he did. He walked all the way home. In fact, there wasn't any rubber left on the bottom of his shoes. His feet were completely swollen and bloody. But he made it home just over a day ago, and he's been sleeping ever since.

Me: Wow! So, he never called for a ride? Not a single call?

Jose's wife: Nope. When Jose sets his mind on something, he just does it.

Me: I'd say so! Well, unless it's to go to work!

True story. I'll add more when he wakes up and calls us back. 😶

05/23/2017

Me: Jason, I never got your application. I know you have been out of work since February.

Driver: Yes, Sir, I need a job bad. I'm broke and losing my place to live right now!

Me: We have a few jobs available there. We just needed the rest of your work history to proceed.

Driver: Oh, yes! That's right, I forgot!

Me: Let's just do it over the phone then, and we can get you started.

Driver: I have to call you back. I am at the bank applying for a loan to get a new boat!

Me: Priorities, right?

12/27/2017

Driver: Sorry I haven't returned your call. I don't usually keep my phone anywhere nearby.

Me: Okay, buddy, but that excuse hasn't worked since 2005. SMH [shaking my head].

2018, the Year I Met Henry

02/18/2018

Well, this one takes the cake!

Me: Why did you tell me that you had *no* accidents in the last five years? I just got a report back and it shows you have had seven in the last three years alone!

Driver: I thought you meant like real accidents or wrecks, not those little things.

Me: So, you do not consider hitting and totaling a parked vehicle an accident? Or running your truck and trailer down the entire side of a three-hundred-foot building an accident? Are you serious? Can you explain what's minor about these before we discuss the other five you failed to mention?

I am so glad it's Friday and I am out of here!

04/08/2018

Monday morning report:

Driver "Bob" was removed from the property because he was refusing to take his drug test and became hostile towards staff members when he was asked to give a reason why he was declining the test.

The driver was then asked to leave orientation and vacate the company property and hotel. Before leaving, he proceeded to yell and then thew a chair which bounced off a window almost hitting another staffer.

Driver "Bob" proceeded back to his hotel room where he gathered his belongings. Before vacating the hotel property, however, he moved everything that was inside the hotel room to the outside. By everything, we mean even the shower curtain.

04/29/2018

Me: What's your name? I will pull you up.

Driver: Henry [then shouts]. DJ Valor the Party Rocker Vonson!

Me: Great! So, it's Henry Vinson? Give me a sec to pull you up.

Driver: No! [he interrupts me clearing his throat loudly through the phone.] It's Henry [shouts the rest] DJ VALOR THE PARTY ROCKER VINSON! Bam Boom! [Inaudible heavy metal scream.]

Me: Okay Henry, is that your legal name?

Driver: Yes, I had it changed to [shouting] HENRY DJ VALOR THE PARTY ROCKER VINSON!

Me [myself interrupting this time]: I got it. Please do not scream in the phone again. I can hear you, and we are not in the club.

After we got through everything, I had to call him back. I got his voice mail that proclaims his name again as, Henry DJ Valor the Party Rocker Vinson Bam boom, along with some crazy music. Four minutes later, I left my message asking if I needed to add "Bam Boom" after his name.

09/19/2018

Tim was a CDL school candidate.

Me: Hey, Tim, I got everything set up for Monday. Did you get by the DOT doc for your updated physical?

Tim: Yes, Sir.

Me: Okay, and did you get a two-year DOT physical?

Tim: Well, they denied me all together.

Me: Denied? What for? I have down no medical restrictions, no meds, and even the fact that you said you didn't need glasses.

Tim: Well, they denied me because you have to have 20/40 vision. I am completely blind in my left eye and 80% blind in my right.

Me: [silence]

Tim: You there?

Me: Yes. Did you not know you were completely blind before today?

Tim: Yes, but I still have a lot of my peripheral vision. I figured it wouldn't be an issue.

Me: Tim, first question. If you were to be behind the wheel driving an eighty-thousand-pound tractor trailer, do you think it would be important to be able to see what is in front of you?

10/22/2018

Driver: I'm not sure that's going to work.

Me: So, getting home every day on the day shift with weekends off and a minimum of $1,100 a week with benefits isn't enough?

Driver: Nah. I just can't do it.

Me: How much money have you made since you became unemployed back in March, eight months ago?

Driver: None.

Me: You are saying you have *not* made one dollar in the last eight months? How are you paying your bills like rent and such?

Driver: I am living at home with my mom.

Me: You are living at home with your mom at the age of fifty-six?

Driver: That's right.

Me: Let's forget about everything else for a moment and just think about this.

With this job, you would have made over $30,000 since you became unemployed, but instead you made $0 and are willing to continue doing so?

Driver: If that's what I have to do.

Me: You cannot think that this really makes sense. Call me when you are ready to go to work.

12/09/2018

This isn't driver related, but I came across it while putting together this book, Drivers' Dilemmas. Ariel is my daughter and it was funny so I thought I would share it.

Me: Ariel, grab me a Phillips head screwdriver out of my toolbox.

Ariel: Okay, Dad, I'll be right back!

After about six or seven minutes, Ariel returned.

Ariel: Dad, I couldn't find a Phillips, but I found and brought back a few Stanleys.

An Eventful 2019

03/06/2019

It's hard to beat a day when you get a call like this one last week. Most of you see the funny and weird crap I deal with and not all the great calls I get. So, I wanted to share one of the more positive moments that keeps me doing what I do and loving it.

First a little backstory on Johnny. Johnny, who is from Northwest Arkansas, walked into my office in downtown Rogers back in March of 2011.

He started off saying, "I am sorry to waste your time and bother you all, but no one will help me and I saw your office sign walking by and I don't know... I just thought..."

Evelyn greeted him, and I walked up as he proceeded to tell us how he was down on his luck, penniless, alone, couch surfing, and no one would hire him for one reason or another. He was getting denied for everything from not having an address, the length of time since he had graduated CDL school, too much unemployment, and much more. Well, he finally came to the right place. After a little work, we got him driving and into his first driving job on April 15, 2011.

Six months later (10/2011), we moved him to a great company where he has been ever since, proving to be a great asset. Which brings us to the call I received this day in March of 2019.

After catching up on some chitchat with Johnny, we started discussing his job and how it's been going.

Johnny: Well, that's actually why I was calling you today. I just wanted to share with you that as of Friday at midnight, I will have had my one millionth dollar deposited into my account from this job that you got me seven-and-a-half years ago. You guys changed my life and gave me a chance when no one else did.

These are the stories that best explain why we do what we do.

09/29/2019

I cannot believe people fall for this, but I have a driver who ended up homeless, losing his car and his trailer. And now, he's being investigated by Homeland Security all because he was giving money to a "girl" he had never met outside of Facebook.

This "girl" messaged him on Facebook and they began chatting.

Fast forward and she texted claiming that she was dying of cancer and in a hospital. She needed money for her treatments. So, she asked him to send her some money or, better yet, just bring it to her.

He ended up getting routed through the hospital in L.A. where she claimed to be. Of course, when he arrived, she was too ill to see him, so he left the money in the lobby and left the hospital.

As he walked back out to the truck, the FBI was waiting for him. As it turned out, this woman was actually a terrorist and they thought that he was contributing to her cause.

11/19/2019

A great way to either upset one hundred truck drivers or get them to call you back.

Accidentally, group them all together in a text message with each other.

I believe this group text is still going on to this day. LOL!

12/05/2019

It may be hard to believe, but this is an all-too-common story we come across.

Some people just won't take a job even if it they're getting paid to sit on the couch and watch television. The conversation I had at 1:17 p.m. went a lot like this:

Me: Okay, let's go back over this. So I can better understand, are you saying that you will only start at a company that has a one-day orientation? And you think you will have a delay getting your first check if not?

Driver: Yes, Sir, that's right. If I am sitting, I am not making no money.

Me: It's a paid orientation.

Driver: I know, but I am still sitting. You know how it is, man.

Me: Let me ask you this, then. How long have you been sitting at the house without a job?

Diver: Just about seventy-five days this go 'round.

Me: And how many checks this past seventy-five days have you gotten waiting for that opportunity with a one-day orientation?

Driver: Zero. So far, none.

Me: [silence]

Driver: You there? You still there... hello?

Me: Yes, Sir, I am. I'm just letting all that math we did settle for a minute.

12/13/2019

My text: Did you make it home? Because if you want to start working by next week and have a check on Friday, you need to sign the application.

Driver text: Hello. Yes, I got in. I am in OKC. Got here about 2:30 a.m. Have not done the application yet because I need the perfect fit. Things are good for me right now, so I can hold out a minute.

What I am looking for is something that's going to be paying money and not spending time training because my water is turned off, my electric is off, and my car was picked up for repo.

My text: You said things are good for you?

12/18/2019

This has to be the strangest "reason for discharge" ever put on an application. I got it this past week and it read:

 I was NOT technically terminated. My x-wife put Meth in my CPAP machine so I'd inhale it without knowing it! Then, she called into my work and told them I had been doing Meth as revenge for me getting her kicked out of my house.

Truth be told, I was already quitting the same day they were drug testing me, so I wasn't technically fired for the failed drug test. Plus, it wasn't my fault. Please call my mamma at 555-555-5055 and my sister over at 555-555-5505 as proof because she admitted what she did to me and to them. Thank you for your consideration.

12/12/2019

On today's episode of "important things not worth mentioning when trying to be rehired by a company":

Company sends this back on an employment verification: This driver was a previous employee who had a wreck in a truck and was arrested for leaving the scene of the accident. The driver did not mention this or list it on the application. Did they not mention any of this to you?

I called the driver.

Me: Good afternoon, is there a reason why you didn't mention that you previously worked for the company where we were going to get you hired? And why you also specifically answered "no" to "have you worked at this company before?"

Driver: It was a while ago and not really worth mentioning.

Me: Let me ask you this. Did you think the company would forget something like that? I mean, usually someone says, "Oh yeah, I worked for them before and it sucked," or "Yeah, it was awesome."

And until now, I would have bet that 100% of those asked about this specific instance would have said:

"Oh yes, I did drive for them. Unfortunately, the last time I worked for them I was arrested after ten police officers and six police cars chased me down in my truck. The truck was impounded, and I was taken to jail."

Something along those lines. It certainly isn't something you forget or think that's "not worth mentioning." We haven't even discussed leaving the scene, the hit and run charge, and the falsifying a police report... which you also all failed to be mentioned!

Come on Friday! LOL.

12/31/2019

This guy's starting the New Year off right!

As usual, here's a little backstory to get you going. For one reason or another, this driver hasn't made it successfully through a few orientations. Mainly, it's for DOT reasons, but now a company that denied him previously offered him a job. The only condition is that he has to return within the next two weeks.

51-year-old driver: I just can't leave right now because there isn't anyone to send money back to. I need someone here at home to pay my bills for me.

(This was after 10 minutes of explaining to me that he doesn't have any money, that he's cold because utilities are off, and that his car notes are late and pending a repo.)

Me: Well, with you out of work at home, how are you paying the bills?

Driver: I'm not. That's why the electric's off. Remember me saying that?

Me: Why don't you just pay these companies directly over the phone or on line with your phone or computer while you are away earning a paycheck?

Driver: Well, I'm so far behind that when I do pay them, I won't have money to eat.

Me: What you are doing now isn't going to get the heat turned on, buddy. Wouldn't you rather get a check sitting in a truck with heat instead of at home in the freezing cold without heat?

Bottom line, he didn't want to leave and with that I was done working for the year.

December was memorable!

On to 2020!

01/13/2020

Evelyn had been going back and forth with a driver "pulling teeth" over his background.

Evelyn: Okay, do you or don't you have a felony?

Driver: Well, I got a felony but it's like six or ten years old.

Evelyn: Okay, moving forward now. Would you like to share that info with me so we can get you to work?

Driver: I don't really know what it was for. I did some jail time, maybe like three or four years, and that was that.

Evelyn: So, you received a felony, went to jail for three or maybe four years, possibly, and don't know or remember why?

After going back and forth some more,
this driver also couldn't remember his
recent work history beyond the four
driving jobs in the last three months,
forgot that he had been terminated for an
illegal U-turn, and when asked why he
didn't tell us any of this, he claimed, "I
just didn't remember any of that."

01/17/2020

This next account took place in a text conversation with a driver.

After a twenty-five minute story about his recent sideswipe that wasn't really his fault and that "could have been avoided had the four-wheeler paid attention to him."

Us: USX is trying to reach you, Jim. Have you spoken to them?

Driver: Yes. They want me to run the speed limit which is 65 on that route! NO THANK YOU! I am an 85-mph guy! I'm from Texas and drive 85! All day, each day, I need to know I can go 85 if needed. Hammer down cowboy!

Us: But you live in Missouri now?

Driver: Well, yes, you know that.

Us: This just doesn't make any sense.
Please call us.

64

01/27/2020

Driver: No, I am not working. My money wasn't right.

Us: Are you working or making any money now?

Driver: Nope

Us: Were you fired, or did you quit?

Driver: I turned in the truck and quit. My money went from $1,200 a week to about $1,000.

Us: And how much are you making now?

Driver: $0, not a dime.

Us: Understood. And for how long?

Driver: Going on two, maybe three months now.

Us: So, you quit a job that you may have lost $800 in but which would have still made you over $8000, for no job and no income?

Driver: Yup, that's right. No one is going to mess with my money.

Us: Do you realize you just lost $8,800 instead of a possible $800?

Happy Monday!

01/29/2020

It is almost February and this driver has been unemployed since July, 2019. We have sent him a release to sign to get his motor vehicle report and an application that is already completed for him and just needs his signature. What's even better is that we have this for not one, but two companies that both far exceed the driver's expectations and qualifications.

Us: Hi Brian, just reminding you that we still need your application back in order to start you on these jobs.

Brian: I am so sorry. I've been so busy. Just going nonstop!

Us: Oh great, so are you working then?

Brian: Nope, but I need to start ASAP! Like yesterday.

Us: Brian, we sent over the paperwork to you nine days ago and every day you said you've been too busy. If you do not want this job, we will give it to someone else and find something different for you.

Brian: Yes, Sir, I know. I do want the job. I've just been taking care of a few things while I had some time off… being unemployed and all.

Us: And you have been unemployed since when?

[Mind you it is January, 29, 2020]

Brian: Since July, 2019.

01/31/2020

Driver: Hi J! I was calling to see what you got for me!

Us: We are just waiting for your initial application to be completed to see what you would qualify for.

Driver: Well, I have a resume but it's on a floppy disk and the lady that's been helping me hasn't been able to get it on one of those USB things.

Us: A floppy? I haven't heard that term since the 1990s! Just email us the work history or add it to the link we sent you. It's been a month. Don't you want to work?

01/31/2020

And another one:

I have been unemployed since March of 2019 and do not have the time to call a company back during the day. Please call me today at 555-555-5055. I am waiting and eager to get to work!

If you have been unemployed for ten months, how much "catching up" could someone possibly have to do in order not to be able to call back a potential employer?

02/12/2020

After reviewing my morning reports, I noticed a driver that had been out of work for almost a year hadn't shown to his orientation. I was worried, so I reached out.

Me: Hi, I see that the company we have you starting at has you labeled as a "no call no show" today. Are you okay? You didn't go to jail, get sick, or have an accident, did you?

Driver: Ha ha! Yes, I am good. I just have some personal issues that have to be taken care of before I go.

Me: Didn't you confirm on Friday?

Driver: Yes, I did, but I didn't know I would have to get this taken care of.

[We talked for a bit more, but he wouldn't reveal any details about what issues he was dealing with, or if there was anything we could do to help him.]

Me: I'm not sure what "this" is, but I am going to have a hard time understanding, much less explaining, how someone who hasn't worked in almost a year and who was scheduled to start on a local day job, doesn't show up for the job because he didn't have his personal issues taken care of. How much time do you need?

Driver: I'm not sure how long this will take.

Me: You've taken the last year off to take care of your personal stuff and haven't made any progress. There's no way to hold this job indefinitely. Good luck! Call when you are ready to make a paycheck!

02/12/2020

Driver: I have never used drugs, but I can't pass a hair test drug screen.

Me: Why not?

Driver: Because I touched a weed plant one time back in July 2019.

Me: It's February of 2020, you know?

02/18/2020

This incident is after numerous similar conversations with this driver I'll name "Kelly." Kelly suffered from a disease called SLFT or Severe Lack of Follow Through.

Kelly: I'm getting pretty discouraged here. Not sure I will even call anyone else for a job.

Me: What do you mean?

Kelly: I'm being denied everywhere. If it's not for the three or four little tickets, then it's for a DUI back in 1999!

Me: I understand. Have you followed up with the two companies we have you approved at already?

To catch you up as a reader, this driver has been approved at 2 different companies pending his ability to sign an already completed application.

Kelly: No. Like I said, I'm discouraged and tired of wasting my time being denied. Is there an application I need to fill out?

Me: Yes. It is the same one you just need to sign. We sent it on February 3rd, February 5th, February 9th, February 13th, and again the 14th. Surly, you remember?

Kelly: Okay, I will call them all first before I waste time signing the thing.

Me: You can't get a job if you won't put in the effort to sign the application, much less calling either company back. You're already completely approved, this is it.

02/20/2020

Me: These companies are denying you saying you have an accident that you didn't disclose. Any ideas?

Driver: Nope, not really. I have never had an accident.

Me: Are you sure? It just doesn't seem possible that five companies would deny you for an accident if you didn't have one.

Driver: I am not sure if you would really consider this an accident-accident, but I backed into a building. It wasn't terrible, but the back end of the trailer punched straight through the building into an office. That's about it, no injuries or anything.

Me: REALLY? And you wouldn't consider that an accident!?

02/21/2020

Continuation of our driver and the FBI incident from September 2019.

Come to find out, he was cleared of any wrong doing and the FBI explained that the "her" that he was in contact with was actually a scammer from Nigeria he'd never met. He, however, told me that he felt he should still give her money to help her with her legal problems.

Me: If she is in jail with the FBI, then how are you talking to her?

Driver: Well, they let her use the phone, receive cash gift cards, and get Amazon deliveries while in prison!

Me: Let me get this straight. So, the FBI is letting a terrorist receive gifts and talk on a cell phone while in prison? Are you hearing what you are saying? Where are you? What are you doing?

Driver: I'm at Western Union sending money to my girlfriend.

Me: What girlfriend?

Driver: Oh, we met online and we're getting married.

Me: So why does she need money?

Driver: It's so that she can pay the taxes on her huge inheritance.

Min you, he's actually been off for two weeks and has to get an advance to do this. WHAT A MESS!

- The scams on social media are rampant. We hear stories like these often, so please be careful. We filter them off our @CDLhunter social media pages almost daily.

02/27/2020

Gina, a driver, called in today for Evelyn. I spoke to her for a while. She's a very fun and interesting woman to talk to from Central Massachusetts.

When I went to hang up, I asked where she had gotten Evelyn's number from.

She replied that she had a letter from Evelyn dated back from March 2015 and that she had never opened it. All this time, she was using the letter as a bookmark!

Fast forward the conversation and she tells me that she was laid off and couldn't find a job. With the extra time, she decided to organize her home and finally open the letter today to find three of Evelyn's business cards. Who would have guessed that five years later she would call us for a job!

03/05/2020

Driver: I won't do an app because it's just too hard [he wanted to simply send a picture of his work history, which he did and it was blurry with the words "clean as a baby bottom background compared to others."]

Me: Well, I am counting six felonies. Babies typically don't have any, LOL.

Me: No accidents, but it says here that back in 2019 you "came over a hill and plowed into the back of the car."

Driver: Yes, but it was stopped over a hill on the other side. He should have moved, but I still got a ticket for failure to control speed. It was only my trailer that smashed the rear and side of the car.

Me: Do you remember writing down that you were "clean as a baby's bottom?"

03/10/2020

Thomas called in at 8:30 a.m. today to say he was upset that his application wasn't approved.

A little back story:

- As of yesterday, at 4:00 p.m., his license was showing a pending suspension.

- He asked that the company not run his information until he cleared it up.

Continuing with the call...

Thomas: I think that the suspension may finally be cleared up. I feel the company should schedule me to start. Actually, it's only fair if they call me with an offer. I was thinking a sign-on bonus, new truck, and the position of my choice.

Me: Thomas, did I miss something? You had a suspension that we verified with you yesterday at 4:30 p.m. central time. The company is Eastern Time zone. How can you expect them to even know your license is cleared up if you haven't called or sent anything in to us or them showing this?

Thomas: I understand, but they should have me hired and ready to drive out pending my proof.

Me: Thomas, where are you now?

Thomas: I'm just leaving the DMV. I just got them to fix my license not a minute or two ago. The whole thing is a racket! What do I need to do Boss?

Me: Now we wait for the system to update in order to get you a job, since you literally are just getting it cleared up as we speak.

03/24/2020

Here's a new "reason for leaving" a job that was put on an application. I hope this one is not going to become a common one in our future.

Reason for leaving:

"Covid19 caused my son to become quarantined and, therefore, our entire family was also. I was on home time when he tested positive so I was also quarantined. When we were cleared, my employer no longer had a position for me."

05/22/2020

This is the continuation of the saga from February and the FBI incident back in 2019. This is what keeps the day-to-day interesting and moving forward.

I spoke to our driver that was getting scammed by the Nigerian girl. To sum up the first part of our conversation, his Nigerian wife (yes, they're apparently somehow married now) is still being investigated by the FBI. But now, he also claims that he is a Facebook contest winner for $650,000 and that his winnings are waiting for him in Lubbock, Texas. All he has to do is to pay the taxes for the winnings and then he will receive the address to where he can pick up his money. Yes, he actually believes that he will be receiving $650,000 in cash once he gets there.

Based on this, he has decided to quit his job or may be getting fired for going there since he has gone out of route.

Me: Have you ever met your wife or even verified these winnings?

Driver: Not yet, and this is the same girl. She is out of the hospital now.

For those who haven't read the previous entries about this driver, he has been investigated by the FBI for his relationship with this woman because he keeps sending her all his money! This "wife" is tied to terrorism. Terrorists fund themselves through scams like this.

Me: I don't understand how all these "women" rope you into these scams and I cannot rope you into a good legit high-paying job!

Driver: I don't know where all these women come from!

Me: I do. Iraq and Nigeria!

Me: Tim, here's my deal. When you get to Lubbock and you find yourself parked in front of the Western Union, you have to call me to switch jobs. Please do not try to cash a $650,000 check or you will be talking to the FBI instead of me for a job. I would also suggest verifying all this before continuing any further.

Driver: Deal.

To be continued, yet again. I hate hearing this!

- The scams on social media are rampant. We hear stories like these often so please be careful. We filter them off our @CDLhunter social media pages almost daily.

09/28/2020

I could totally tell that this guy was trying to hide something.

Me: So, I'm confused. I can tell you aren't being completely truthful here. Did you quit or were you let go?

Driver: Well, actually, I was let go for being uninsurable.

Me: That's a biggie. Explain more please.

Driver: Well, one time I was backing at a truck stop and I hit the corner of a truck. I had thought I just jerked the clutch a little, so I hammered down a bit and tore the bumper, fairings, and quarter of the trailer off. But that was on private property, so it didn't count as an accident — I thought.

Me: Okay, so … [he interrupts]

Driver: ...and there was a time while making a right turn I drove over a bunch of signs. BUT, I only did it to avoid hitting a bunch of cars.

Me: How did your company know if there wasn't a police report?

Driver: Well, the local authorities were looking for me. I was pulled over... well, I had to find a safe place to park I mean, so they gave me fleeing and leaving the scene in a commercial vehicle. I have those tickets pending.

Me; Look, you need to be honest or I can't and will not help you! If you hit a ton of signs to avoid hitting cars, then you would have stuck around to talk to the police and not fled...

Driver: Okay, I'm sorry. Let's start from the beginning.

Me: No, let's have you send me accident reports, MVR, tickets, and look at three years out from now...

09/30/2020

Evelyn and I opened our downtown Rogers, Arkansas, office in March, 2011. We had been open for only an hour and a half when we had our first walk-in driver. He smelled of tobacco, had a cowboy hat on, and turquoise jewelry. He had driven over an hour to get to our office without even calling first. He had a HUGE ear to ear smile and big teary, but hopeful eyes. I could tell he had been crying.

I remember hearing Luke, one of my recruiters, yelling, "Mincke! Mincke! You got someone here."

Evelyn offered him some coffee, Luke took his application, and I chatted for a good hour with him. I remember him saying how he had made his way by taxi [which was VERY hard back then in Northwest Arkansas!] all the way from Gentry for a job he didn't get.

Well, we got him hired at the same company he is still working for today. Mr. JW called me to say that he hit his million miles last month. This week, he gets a new semi to drive with a special paint scheme of his choosing, a jacket, a personalized ring and a watch, a $10,000 longevity bonus, and a second for .01 cents X 1 million SAFE miles logged, which is another $10k. He just wanted to thank us for giving him a chance when no one else did and offer us a steak dinner when he's back in town.

Until next time

I love days like that last September 30th. Those are the days that remind me of the relationships we built and that the struggle and hustle we have gone through is worth it. I love being able to help people find better jobs which meet their goals as well as the needs and wants of their families.

Throughout the years, we have had the honor of placing tens of thousands of drivers and the pleasure of staying in touch with so many of them. We take pride in getting to know each driver on an individual basis as a person and, BEST of all, I've had the incredible blessing to have been able to do it every single day with my best friend and wife, Evelyn!

— *Jeremy Mincke*